Distant Echoes

A Dream Of Life

Copyright Notice

Distant Echoes - A Dream Of Life
© 2021, by Jakob Fox. "All rights reserved."

Written by Jake Fox in addition to:
The Distant Echoes Album

"No part of this document may be reproduced or transmitted in any form or by any means, electronic, mechanical, photocopying, recording, or otherwise, without prior written permission of Jakob Fox."
ISBN: 978-1-6780-8141-6

To the dreamers,
sleeping through their days and only
dreaming through their nights.

"You can be the architect of your own life"

A Short Story
Written By Jake Fox

In Addition To
The Distant Echoes Album

Distant Echoes

A Dream Of Life

Chapter One : The Architect Of Dreams

Chapter Two: All I Ever Wanted

Chapter Three: In The Midst

Chapter Four: Moonlight

Chapter Five: To Sail Across The Sun

End Note

Lyrics

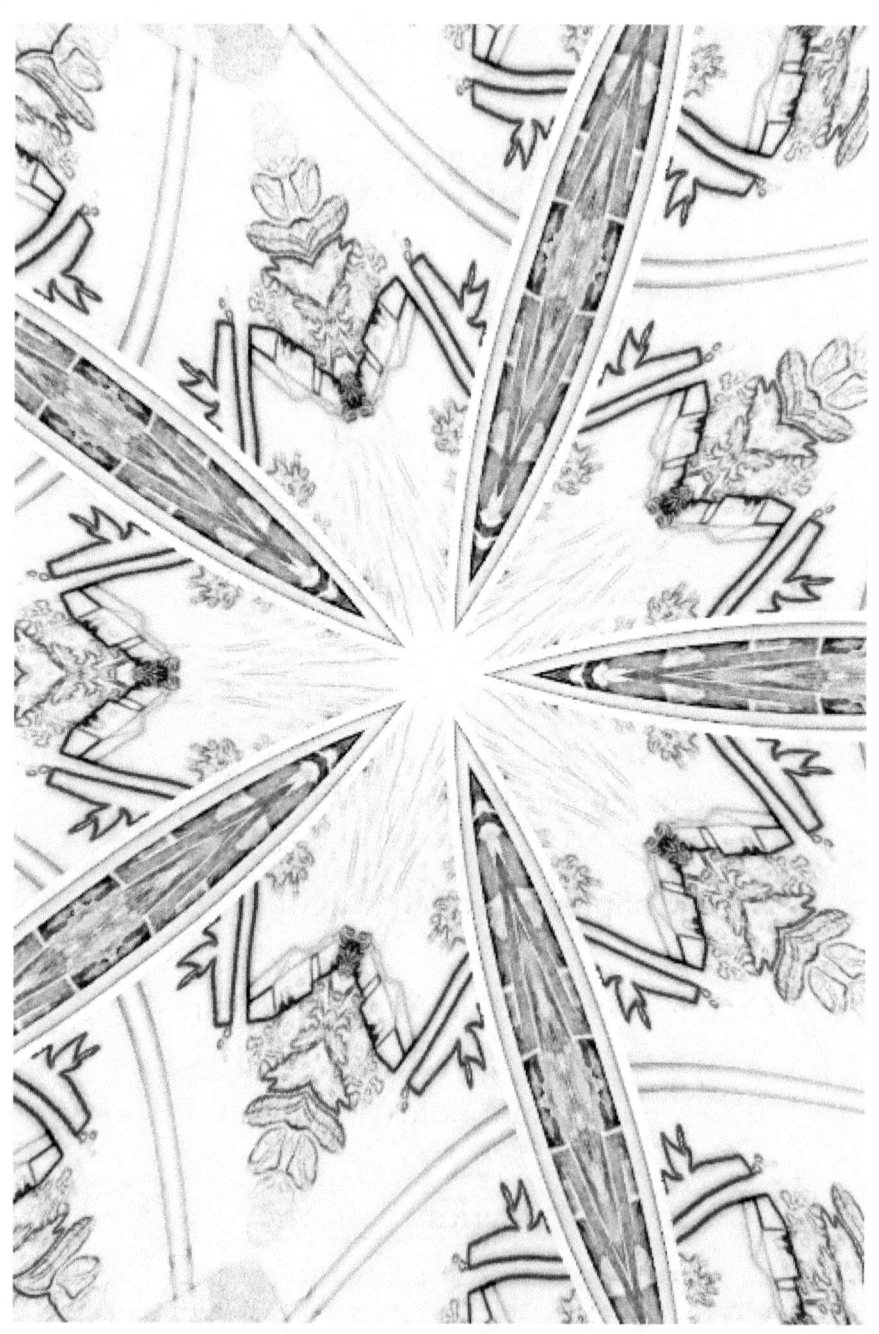

Chapter One

The Architect Of Dreams

As a tranquil ambience emerged, the architect was awoken to find himself lying in a dark room. The branches of a rainbow eucalyptus tree swayed outside and rustled on the windows of the small wooden house he presided in.

The main canvas was midnight black and his surroundings were all painted with watercolours and neon lights. The emptiness and space wasn't something he was accustomed to. Although, it was refreshing to have so much control right from the beginning of the dream.

Whenever he arrived somewhere, no matter what the setting, he knew who he was.

He was 'The Architect Of Dreams'. His job was to weave the dreams and make the transition for the lives in-between.

"Okay, a painted dream. I can work with this."

He sat up in the middle of the room, crossed his legs, and closed his eyes. As he took three deep breaths, he sat in silence listening for the vibration of the dream. By finding the energy source, he could let it fill his body completely and use it like an echo, sending it back out with the fusion of his own essence.

The house started to tremor and the door flew open like a guillotine as he threw the colours from his body. First a sun in the sky was sculpted, then the colours swam through the space, creating land around the house, rocky cliff faces, and a black shore line as far as he could see.

As the architect walked out of the door, he shot the sun and watched in passion. A mix of colours leaked out of the great ball in the sky, dripping like paint. He then took them in his hands, shaped them in a fluid motion, and threw them back, creating an elegant moon to illuminate the setting. With the remaining energy he had, he formed an ocean for the rest of his colours to sleep until he needed them.

He observed the structure of his newest design and began to walk down the shoreline with a mind full of thoughts.

Something still seemed very ominous about the fabrication of this dream. He had never been given a canvas so blank to start with before. Despite it's empty foundation, he had filled it with his design and yet, it still felt as though there was something absent.

As the architect's thoughts grew, the colours began to swirl, producing small waves on the shore.

The frequency resonated in his mind. It was such a familiar sound, but he had no idea from where and which memory it came. He had never created waves before so how could he possibly recognise this sound?

The architect walked further down the beach to a rocky cave where he sat. He mused over his work in deep reflection, connecting his thoughts to the natural flow of the waves. They crashed on the beach with a gaining intensity, sweeping the sand of the shoreline back and forth in an intoxicating motion.

"If there is something missing, why can I not create it? This just doesn't seem right."

There was a haunting feeling inside his being that he had never experienced in any of his previous designs.

He was a perfectionist and the best at what he did.

Why was this time any different?

What was so unbalanced about this dream?

He continued to wonder in awe and couldn't stop thinking about a solution to fix the stability of the dream. However, he had no idea what actions he could deliberate to alter its current state.

If he interchanged the colours it could potentially change the flow of where the dream was going, but the balance would still remain the same. If he duplicated the dream and inverted the colours, he may be able to parallel the two dreams together, but then there would be a risk of the balance slipping even further out.

Whilst in a dither of internal conflict, the colours of the ocean had started to violently collide together and the water was now edging closer towards the architect. Still, he looked to the moon with his mind too occupied to notice the waves pulling the sand away from underneath his toes. In an instant, one single wave embraced the entire shoreline.

The architect arose to his feet, desperately clinging to the edge of the cave wall. The water quickly advanced up his legs, progressing to the waist, and then as high as his chest. With a turn of the tide, the water engaged the architect and started to draw him in.

He tried to counter the swell by pulling the colours back towards him into his clutches, but he had spent so much of his energy on his thoughts that he was easily swept out to sea. Calmly, he spread his limbs and sank to the ocean floor in peace.

The total darkness was soothing to the architect. Lines resembling small jelly fish swam past him, blinking green and purple fluorescent lights, sparking and sizzling with streams of electricity.

The architect had created many oceans before, but this was the first time he had seen the inside of one like this. He perused the frame, impressed with his own work.

"It's a different world down here. Like a dream inside a dream."

Just in his vision, he could faintly see the outline of a bottle drifting towards him. Curiously, he took the bottle in his hand.

"Ahh, this must be the imbalance. This is not my creation."

He then closed his eyes and let go of his breath. When he opened them again, he was back on the black shore. Sitting in position, he placed the bottle in front of him on the sand and stared into it. He was relieved to finally be able to repair the balance of the dream and put his mind at peace, but where did this bottle come from?

What was the message inside? Who was it for?

After carefully contemplating his next move, he opened the bottle, laid the message out in front of him, and read the words transcribed on the piece of paper:

"I want to live."

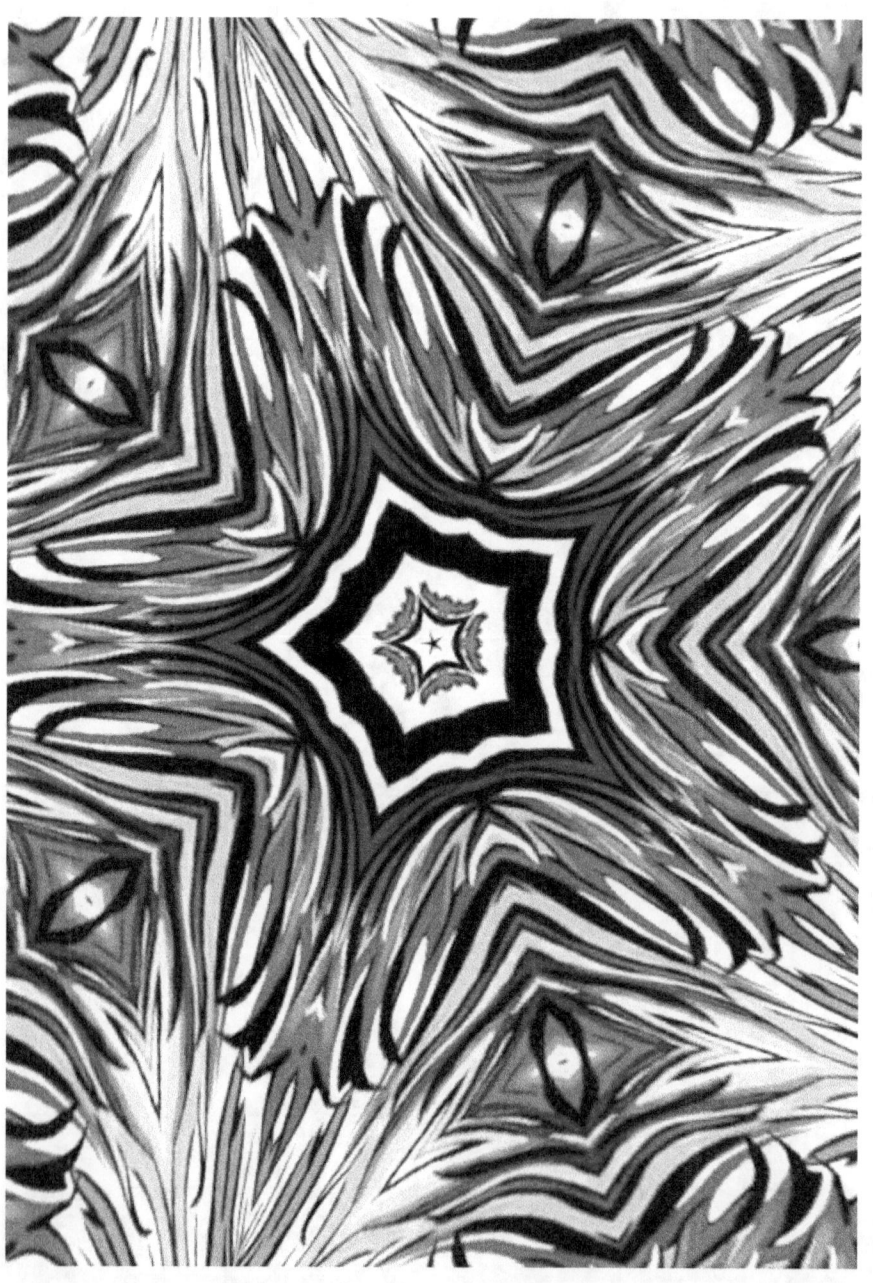

Chapter Two

All I Ever Wanted

The architect sat, mesmerised by these words.

"Where did they come from? What do they mean?"

Language was not a usual theme in his designs, so it was unclear to him as to how this text could have surfaced into this dream.

To the left of his sight, a bridge and a dock formed out to sea. As the architect looked again, he could just distinguish the silhouette of a person sitting at the edge of the dock. He walked out and sat down in front of her.

It was a woman dressed in a white jumpsuit with caramel skin and tied up braids of black and gold. She opened her eyes and gave a glare at the architect. Her eyes were an enigma and the same as that of a lioness, dilating in and out as she stared through the architect.

The architect leaned in with a look of suspicion on his face. After a still silence, he put his hand on his chin and began to question the woman.

"Who are you?"

The woman looked to the left, eyes wide open, and replied in a sarcastic tone.

"Whatever do you mean?"

The architect was taken aback. Who was this person that dared to mock his position in this dream? Did she know who he was?

"Well, you're the first person that I have ever met and I want to know what you are?

With a small snicker the woman replied again.

"I don't know what I am, but I like to be called Zarah. I think it suits me. What do you think?"

The architect fell deeply back into his mind.

"Could a name like this suit an image of hers?"

It was hard to tell for him as everything needed to be balanced. There were an infinite number of names that could potentially integrate and intertwine with her persona. For him, naming things was definitely an unjust cause with no significant result to worry about doing in the first place. However, if he had to choose a name it would have to be perfectly balanced with the character.

Zarah laughed and clicked in the architect's face, snapping him out of his stupor.

"Hey! You think too much! Tell me who you are."

This was an easy question for him. He knew exactly who he was and he loved to tell with an egotistical confidence.

"I am 'The Great Architect'. The one who weaves the dreams for all the lives in-between and I am curious as to how you are here because I couldn't have created you."

"Why is that?" Asked Zarah.

"Because I have never experienced time. I have the ability to take memory, colour and vision to construct my design, but to form a complete being with the complexities of life means I have had to live. Which, I have not. So again, it is impossible for you to be here!"

Zarah quickly replied with another question.

"What is it like to create a dream?"

The architect smirked and responded with satire.

"You wouldn't understand the complex nature of what I do, but basically I'm given a canvas and I draw. It's simple because it's who I am, and who I've always been"

Even quicker, Zarah asked her next question.

"How do you know what to draw?"

"It just comes out of me from a familiar place, almost like it's a memory, but I need to materialise it following the motion and guide-lines of where the dream is going."

In the matter of a moment, Zarah gazed deeply into the architect's eyes with an enticing stare and swiftly asked her last question in a whisper.

"How did you get here architect?"

The architect was speechless. He had never had his identity questioned like this before and his being challenged in such depth.

What was more compelling to him was that he had never questioned himself in this way. How was he here? Where was he before he landed in the idle space? He couldn't even remember the last dream that he had manufactured. He always thought that he constructed the area, but how had he been created?

In his ongoing perplexity, Zarah smiled and took his hand.

"Don't worry, it happens sometimes. Let's go!"

The architect was so intrigued by the woman with the lion eyes that he had to follow.

They ran down the black shore line, shouting and spinning as colours formed and separated around their bodies. Laughing and in a daze, they sat on the shore next to each other in a comfortable silence.

"I have a question for you now Zarah. What is it like to live?"

Zarah took a breath, gazed out into the distance of the infinite sea, and replied.

"It takes time to live."

The architect contemplated the connotation of 'time' in this phrase and devised his next question in return.

"Do you know what love is?"

"I don't know what it is, but sometimes I stare off the dock into the swirling colours. I like to think they are looking back at me in the same way that I see them.
You should try it."

The architect could not comprehend what Zarah was implying with this answer, but in the pursuit of finding some significance to this conversation he decided to act upon her words. What was there to lose?

He walked to the edge of the dock and stared at the swirl of colours. In an echo he was lost within the words of the message he had found earlier.

"I want to live
I want to live..."

In that moment, the architect realised that he had been responsible for creating so many dreams, he had not acknowledged his own.

The one true dream that he ever had.

The desire to live.

He continued to stare, hypnotised by the colours as they moulded and isolated, forming magical patterns and mandalas. Sparks flew past him in a surge of voltage, and all light and sound distorted together into one.

In a thunderous clap, the architect lost his breath, fainted, and fell off the dock into the sea.

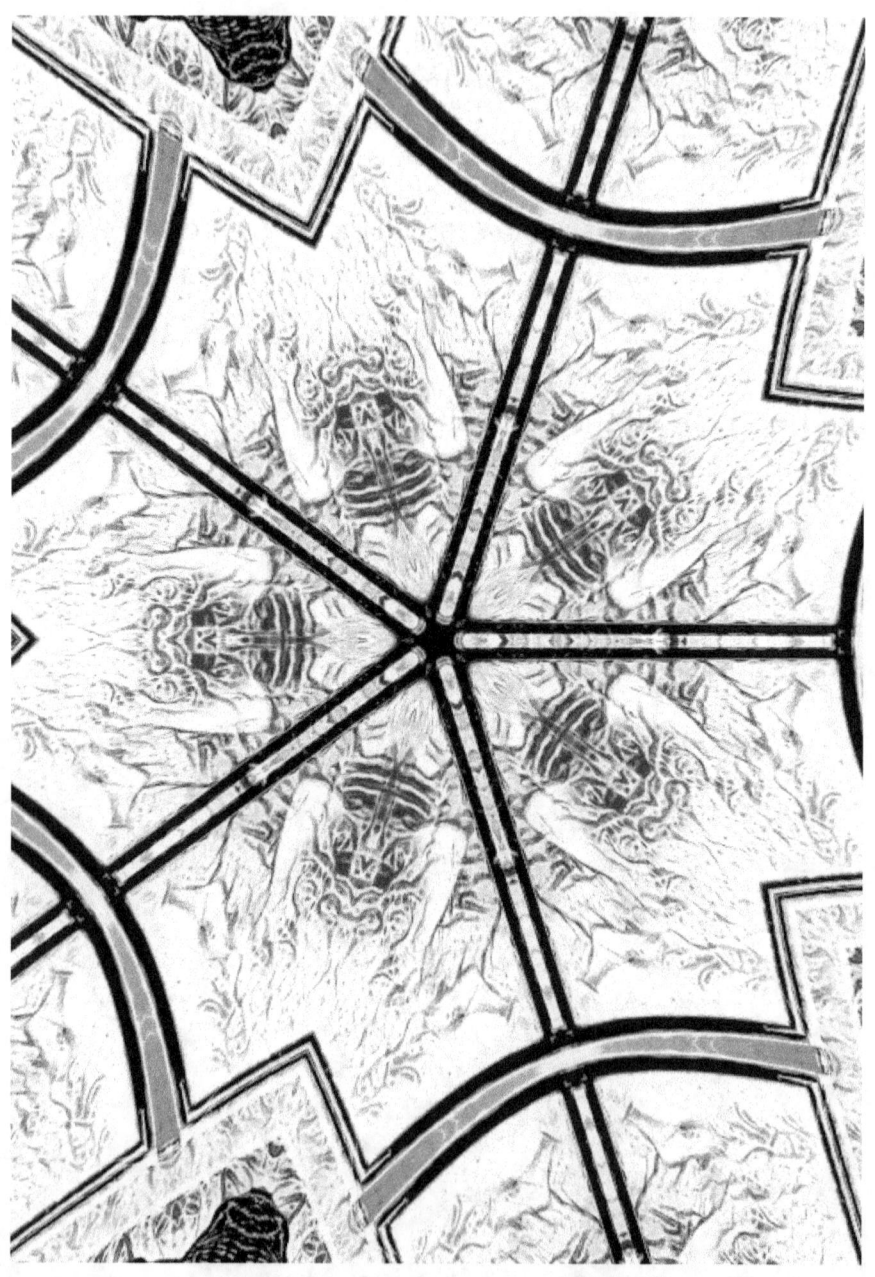

Chapter Three

In The Midst

The architect launched himself up, opening his eyes and gasping for air.

"Wow, that was a strange one! It doesn't matter now, time for work."

Compared to most of his other dreams, this one had many more complexities. As he got out of bed, he realised that he was undressed. He changed into a loose white top and black track pants.

He wandered through the scene and discovered that he was in a cosy one bedroom apartment. Plants and natural decorations displayed through the space and photographs of various people were framed and fixed to the walls. In the main room, there was an old record player with vinyls spread out across the floor. To the side of the room, there was a balcony decorated with more plants, and a shaded table and chairs. He then approached the window and opened the curtains to reveal a magnificent view of the city.

This was even more peculiar than his last design. The previous dream that he awoke in was an empty canvas, where this one seemed quite full with less work to do. However, the architect never questioned his job before and decided it was time to get started.

He sat on a Persian rug in the middle of the living room, closed his eyes, and started to breathe. He listened to the sounds of the city, felt the pulse of the room, and searched for the in and out vibration to start weaving the dream and casting the colours.

Suddenly, he was shocked by a loud knock on the door. He opened the door to find an empty hallway with a glass elevator.

"Again, not exactly what I'm used to, but let's see where this goes."

He walked into the elevator and the lights automatically switched on unravelling patterns of black and gold. The door then closed and he dropped down to the ground floor. He walked out of the elevator, past the open doors of the building, and through the tall front gates, leading him to the road.

For the first time in his known existence, he could really sense his surroundings. The warm caress of the sun, the aroma of freshly brewed coffee, the sound of brass instruments echoing through the streets, and the beautiful ambience of language.

He was so used to creating, but never having the time to feel his designs.

"What is this land?"

As he walked the pathways to the centre of the city, people flashed past like speeding lights. The architect waited to be stopped, but to his surprise, the people just stared down at their devices. They briskly walked past, not acknowledging him at all.

"Why don't they see me? I am 'The Great Architect' that created this land and they shift around me like I am one of them."

The architect stood puzzled in the middle of the path as people continued to move in a busy shuffle.

"It's a very odd coincidence. This dream is full of people directly following my last dream meeting Zarah. This must be a continuation, but who are they?"

As the sun started to fall and beam its orange light through the gaps of overhead skyscrapers, the architect felt a chill race down his spine and small bumps emerge all over his skin like braille.

"I need to find the apartment again."

He began to walk back at a pace to where he had come from. He entered the front gate and proceeded through the glass doors of the building once again.

A young man dressed in casual, surf style clothes quickly passed by and openly took a hold of the architect's shoulder on his way out.

"Hey, you should head up to the roof and check out the scenery. It's unreal. I'll be back up soon!"

The architect turned and stepped into the lift. The glass doors closed instantaneously and the golden elevator took him to the top of the building.

As he walked out to the rooftop, he could see so clearly. The view was astonishing and in his vision were all the shades of colour that he had used in every one of his designs. The sky was indigo, orange, and pink. There were buildings of green, yellow, and navy. The streets were grey, white, and black, filled with the lights of people walking together in one image of synchronicity.

The architect sat on the edge of the building, his legs hanging off the side. He closed his eyes and started to calmly breathe, relaxing his mind.

Behind him, he heard the sound of steps approaching and the man he had met earlier appeared out of the glare from the last few rays of sunlight.

The man dropped his bag on the ground and sat next to the architect on the ledge.

"It's really something up here, hey?"

The architect looked out to the city and replied.

"Yeah it is. I could design something truly amazing from this view."

"Oh, so you're a designer? It's nice to meet another creative."

"Actually, I am 'The Architect'. I am the one who weaves the dreams for the lives in-between, but I'm a little confused about what's happening in this one. Who are they down there?"

"They are the lonely dreamers. Sleeping through their days and dreaming through their nights. More interested in the life of their devices, rather than the life in front of them."

The architect was reminded of the imbalance he felt in his last dream and formed a question for the man he had just met on the rooftop.

"What is loneliness?"

The man delayed his answer, grabbed two drinks from his bag, gave one bottle to the architect, and began to drink from the other one. He then pointed down to the city below, loosely gripping the neck of the bottle in his hand.

"Down there is a sea of colours all caught in a midst, just bouncing off one another. Always asking impossible questions and never receiving an answer. They don't search, they just wait. It's difficult to sail against the current of time, watching the colours go past. All you can do is hope that you're going the right way."

The architect stepped down from the ledge and walked to the middle of the rooftop. The man then stood up, balancing on the edge of the building, facing the architect.

"Where are we?" Asked the architect.

The man didn't answer, but started moving his body in a trance like fashion, dancing and stumbling.

He then responded with a drunken phrase.

"It seems like you need a change of scenery. You should get out of this place."

"Where would I go? How do I leave?"

The man smiled and pointed to the architect.

"How did you get here?"

With a confused look, the architect quietly replied.

"I don't remember."

"Then why does it matter how or where you go, so long as you're ready?"

The man took one last drink from his bottle and stopped moving his body about, standing completely still in place. He closed his eyes, drew one deep breath, and free fell off the back of the ledge.

The architect ran forward to see the horrific scene on the other side below. To his surprise, there was nothing but the traffic of the people, flowing with the nature of the roads.

A hypnotising vision, much alike to the colours off the edge of the dock.

The architect knew then that he was ready to go.

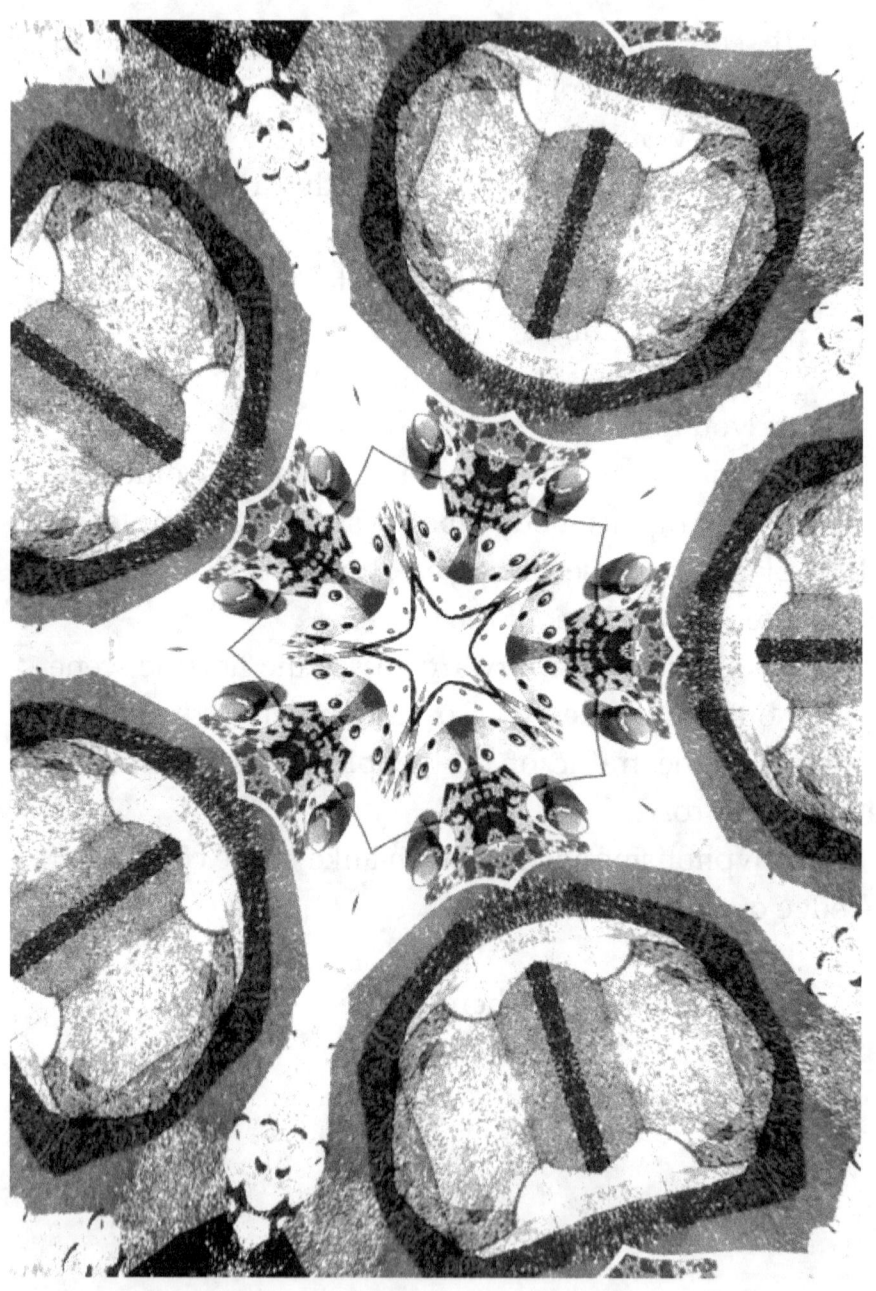

Chapter Four

Moonlight

In one big wave of turbulence, the architect hit his head on the window to his side and awoke to the sound of the bus' engine slowing. The wheels were turning to the right and sliding the rocks and gravel of the road underneath the tyres of the bus.

The architect had been travelling on this bus for three consecutive days. He had been sleeping during the days and had not seen the sun once. At night he had been awake, staring through the same window. The only views were the curves of the mountains reflecting the luminescence of the moon, and a road of light posts guiding the way to the next destination.

In the early morning of the third day, the bus halted to a stop and the doors slid open.

A black haired woman wearing a red backpack, a green trench coat, and denim jeans got on the bus.

Up until this moment, the architect was the only person to be travelling on the bus, so he was interested to find out more about this new arrival.

The woman approached him and asked if she could sit in the seat opposite.

"Of course," said the architect, gesturing with his hand to the seat.

The woman sat down, took a book from her bag and started to write. As the architect gave a glance to his side at the woman, he noticed a name on the book. Izabela.

"Hey Izabela, What are you doing?"

The woman continued to write. She was already seduced by the pages of her notebook. After some time, she replied in a shy manner.

"I'm a writer, but it's a difficult profession. I've never left the city before and I need to get away. I'm a fugitive of time and I can't wait anymore. I need to live, to find the inspiration to write."

She slowly closed her book, put her pen down, and turned to face the architect.

"Where are you going?" She asked.

"I've just been on this bus trying to find the right time to get off."

Izabela smiled, picked up her bag, and put her book back inside.

"Does this feel like a good time?"

As the bus stopped at the top of a hill, they left and started walking down to a beach in the distance.

Izabela kicked her feet along the edge of the water and looked across to the architect.

"Hey, I didn't ask who you were?"

The architect was overwhelmed. He had gone through so much pressure in his last few dreams that he couldn't think of an appropriate answer anymore. He was always so sure of himself, but for the first time, looking at this new person in front of him, he felt like he could be anyone.

"I thought I was 'The Architect', but now I'm a little confused."

Izabela smiled and laughed, staring him down.

"The only architect?"

"Well, who do you think I am?"

Izabela thought of her answer and formulated it just as diligently as the architect would.

"I think we project roles onto people, fitting them into our lives the way we need them to and not always in the way that suits their true expression. However, first you need to decide who you are in your own dimension before anyone can do it for you."

The architect started to think about this response as he trailed behind. He had never thought about the lives of the dreamers. He was always solely focused on the structure of the dream. Sometimes he didn't even notice the dreamers in his designs.

Izabela was already running ahead when she suddenly turned and shouted back to the architect.

"Hey a house!"

They investigated the beach house, finding letters scattered across the table and black and white pictures framed on the wooden shelves. It seemed as if no one had lived in the house for a lifetime.

"Let's stay here tonight," Izabela said excitedly.

As Izabela relaxed on the deck, the architect went back down to the shore. He walked into the water and let his body soak in the salt of the sea. As he picked up the white sand, the feeling of it just slipped away off his body and tingled against his skin like electricity. In the distance, the sun was starting to flirt with the horizon.

He ran back up to the house to meet Izabela and dried his hair with a towel as he sat on the edge of the deck. The sky transformed with colors of pink and orange, and the echoes of the waves filled the house, sweeping back to the sea with a cool breeze. The couple sat side by side, looking out to the ocean.

"So, what type of architect were you? Did you design houses like this one?

"Yeah I did, but I was more the type to create a scene. With a single shot I could shoot the sun and watch it fall down."

The architect gave the gesture with his finger of shooting a gun to the sun exactly when the last bit of light slipped behind the horizon.

"I was 'The Architect'. I weaved the dreams for the lives in-between."

Izabela gave a small laugh and pushed his arm to the side.

"Did you ever wonder where the sun went?"

"Actually, I never did. I always had the moon for company."

Izabela leaned forward, clenching her hands underneath her chin. Her eyes lit full of light, reflected by the sky's changing colours.

"What if the moon was at peace and the sun was waiting for you the whole time?"

The night was calm and had a mysterious atmosphere. The light of a full moon illuminated the beach house through its open windows. The only sounds to be heard were the waves crashing gently on the shore.

The architect peacefully awoke on his side to find Izabela in bed, lying in front of him. She gave him a half smile and quietly whispered, "Hey."

He stared into her deep brown eyes, contemplating all the ways his mind had shifted from all the experiences he had lived. He then asked Izabela a question that had been on his mind since the last time he had asked it.

"Izabela. Do you know what love is?"

Izabela took a breath, put her hand on his face, and answered his question.

"The problem is that you looked at the colours and not into them. It's about stopping the colours, and showing them that you truly see them for what they are. It's finding a unique piece of them that no one else in the universe can see and letting them fall for that piece of themselves that they can see in only you. Then, you must recognise that the piece is yours and hold it close to your heart so you never let it go."

The architect rolled on his back. He felt a hollow running through his body, but also a sense of reassurance as he laid by Izabela.

"Architect. If you create the dreams for the lives in-between, can you tell me what happens when you die?"

The architect had dreamed of living for so long that he had never thought about the notion of death. He stared at the ceiling and quietly responded.

"I don't know. I haven't died before."

Izabela gently took the architect's wrist and smiled.

"Hmm, well you should know. I like the way you look at me."

As he turned to his side, the hologram of Izabela faded into stardust. His mind, like glass, shattered into millions of particles. He had never felt sorrow like this before. The sense of her grasping hand was still present on his wrist, the smell of her essence was still infused on the pillow beside him, and her presence still flowed throughout the house.

The architect got out of bed and frantically ran to the shore. The only thing on his mind were the echoes of Izabela's words.

"What if the sun is waiting for me?"

He dragged a small sailboat into the water, laid in the bottom of the hull, and began to drift away with the current.

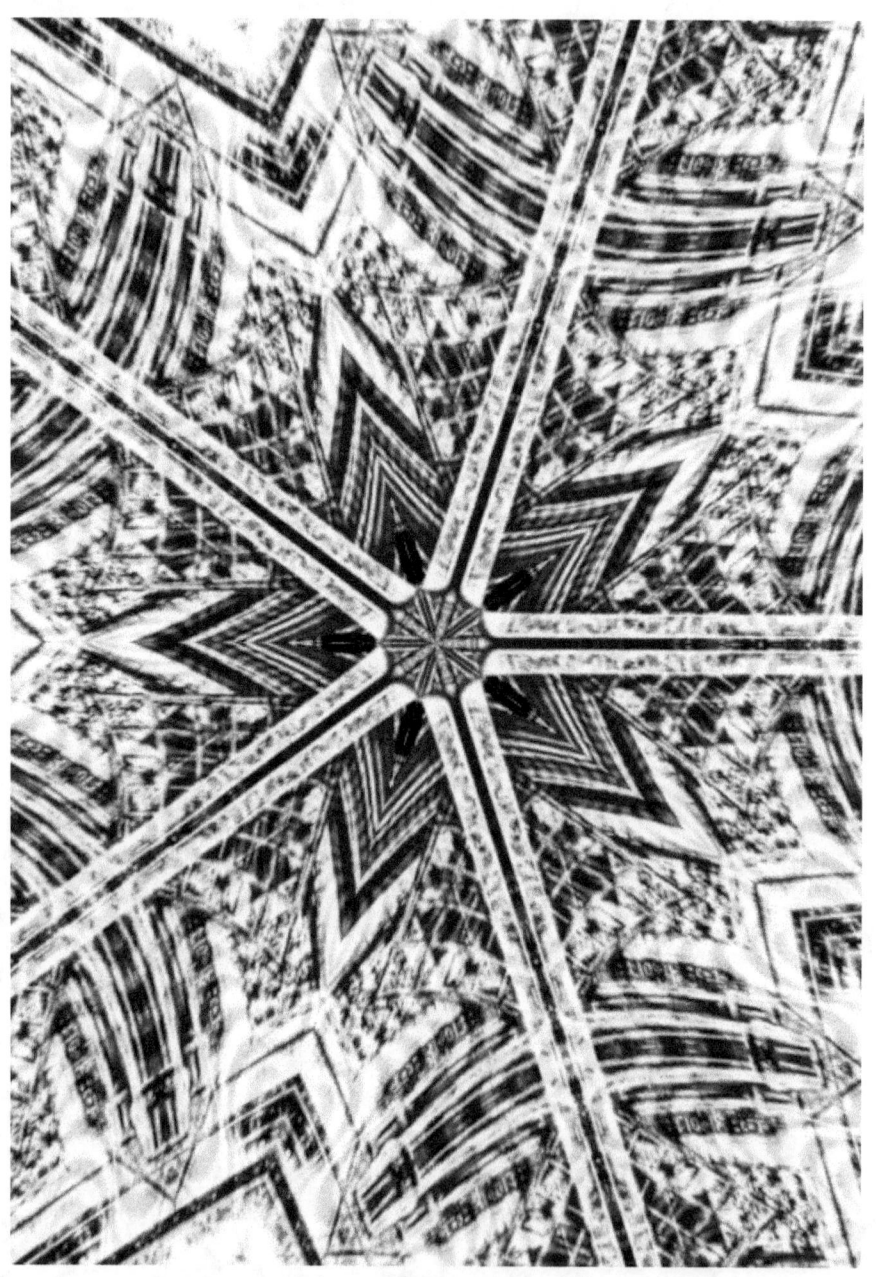

Chapter Five

To Sail Across The Sun

As the architect opened his salt coated eyes, the boat gently rocked side to side with the sound of splashing water hitting against its edges.

Hopelessly, he sat up to find himself in the middle of the ocean with the sun bearing down upon his body.

He ripped the tiny sail down and tied it to the front of the boat's deck to make a shade for himself. He then tore his shirt to create a mask from the sun.

The architect shouted to the sky in despair.

"Why is time essential? If we know what is to become, then what is the significance of living?"

He pondered everything that had happened to him. The black shore, the man from the rooftop, and the woman on the bus.

He looked to the sky and thought about all the dreamers.

"Who were they? What were their lives like?"

"What did they dream of?"

He searched the ocean and began to notice the vastness of his surroundings. It was just him and the sun. He smiled, looking up to the flare of light in the sky.

"So this is where you wait."

The sunlight reflected off the water and a swirl of colors surrounded the boat. The architect looked through the colors only to realise that he had found exactly what he was searching for. He had finally lived his dream.

He tore down the shade and basked in the sun's warmth, feeling every inch of his body come to life.

As he looked back to the boat, he caught sight of a small cabinet under the bow. He unlatched the lock and opened it to discover Izabela's notebook hiding inside, and behind it, the bottle given to him by the man from the rooftop.

The architect sat with his eyes closed and tried to channel the flowing vibration of the sea. When he found it he opened his eyes, took a page from the notebook, and tried to compose a message in the most beautiful and poetic of ways.

He finished writing and revised his work, but realised that it just didn't seem to express the effect he wanted to portray. He threw the note away and took another piece of paper simply writing the words:

"I want to live."

In the hull of the boat he noticed a cork preventing the water from entering the small vessel. He unplugged the seal, rolled up his note, and used the cork to encapsulate the message inside the bottle. He then threw the bottle into the ocean hoping that someone would find it one day.

The boat flooded and submerged itself into the water. The architect closed his eyes and peacefully descended to the bottom of the sea once again.

His mind was empty and his heart content.

When he opened his eyes he found himself washed up, back on the black shore where he began. A song of entrancing dissonance saturated his being, echoing around his drenched body as he came to.

"You look exhausted architect."

The architect sat up to find Zarah sitting in front of him smiling.

"It was a long life," said the architect.

Once again, Zarah glared into his soul with her alluring eyes.

"I need to ask you a question Zarah. What is life?"

Zarah laughed aloud and replied.

"Life is the perfect hallucination. I feel like there may be something else you would rather ask me though?"

The architect then asked the question he had patiently waited a lifetime to understand.

"Zarah, What is a dream?"

Zarah waited to respond, then spoke into his soul.

"A dream is the equilibrium of vibrational energy, pushing and pulling, back and forth like the waves of the ocean. It's the colors between the black and white. The transition of feeling and emotion. It's life and death"

Zarah drew nearer to the architect and rested her forehead on his.

"Thank you for returning architect. I have waited."

The couple closed their eyes, breathing in and out, dissipating in a cyclone with the painted colours that encompassed them.

End Note
Jake Fox Music

What began as a year long trip through South America, then somehow transformed into a short story about an architect and a dream of life.

I left Australia almost instantaneously after completing an album called Tidal Motion. Although I was happy with the outcome of the music, I just felt as if my determination to create something great was dictating the way I was living my life.

Ambition can be a possessive entity that is bittersweet.
It has the ability to push you forward by wanting more from yourself. However, it can also pull you out of living completely in the present.

If you had it all, then what would you want the most? Probably just to live and experience life as it is.

I couldn't shake the feeling that there was something from life I was missing.

I decided that I needed to take a short break from my ambitious music goals and find some real experiences travelling the world.

I travelled through Chile, Peru, Bolivia, and Brazil, adventuring to many amazing places including jungles, mountains, and ongoing coastlines.

I met fascinating people with stories to tell, saw many ocean sunsets, learnt about ancient cultures, challenged myself with new languages and different environments, and tried to live in each moment.

At the same time, there was a lull between the excitement where I could reflect on my thoughts.
I read books, listened to new music, conversed with inspiring humans, connected with nature, and wrote down as many quotes and ideas as I possibly could.

I moved to Curitiba, Brasil, with just my backpack full of clothes and a laptop full of photos and music. I lived in a cosy one bedroom apartment with my partner.

I was very inspired by what I had gained over my experiences that I had an urge to start writing again. I bought a cheap Tagima guitar and started to work on a few ideas.

I began with a song called 'In The Midst'. I wrote most of the lyrics whilst staying in the Amazon, and it was a lot to do about different people's perceptions of life and the strange coincidences that can sometimes alter the directions we take in life.

I continued to write songs, repeatedly changing lyrics, discovering new instrumental ideas, discarding songs, merging others, and constantly updating the project as a whole.

I had most of the lyrics written to 'Moonlight', and different outlines and ideas written to other various songs. However, I felt like the songs just weren't connecting in the way that I had in mind.

The next song I started writing was called 'A Memory In Motion', which eventually changed to "All I Ever Wanted". The song was about creating an escape and a need to seek the greater things that life has to offer. It was inspired greatly by the feeling I had on a trek to Machu Picchu.

I was walking along a path and had to tie my shoelace. As the rest of my group walked ahead I was left by myself walking this path, staring at snow capped mountains, the flowing rapids, and the truly amazing scenery. It was at this moment that I realized I was living the life I always wanted, and the life I knew existed outside the routine life many of us call "reality". However, in a way it was also a taste of the life I wanted to continue to live in the future. Adventuring and exploring the wonders of the world.

As I saw the project coming together, I was content with its direction, but I still felt like something was missing at its core.

I sat down for three days straight, just guitar in hand, and my pen and paper. I wanted to force something out that I knew was hiding inside.

I came up with the chorus for 'The Architect Of Dreams' and then the verses started to flow. I had no idea where the song was going, but I continued to write without thinking too much about it.

I ended up getting more than six pages of messy lyrics out, and pulled them all together to create a song. I read the lyrics trying to figure out the significance of my own creation. Who was this 'Architect Of Dreams'?

I sat on the song for a few days, playing it over and revising the lyrics, when an idea clicked. I could tell the tale of this Architect, by connecting all the songs together into one story-line.

After some contemplation, I took my laptop out and started to write. 'The Architect' who weaved the dreams. Coincidentally, his only dream was to experience life.

I wanted to write with the visions of my explorations in mind, and fuse them with some dream like imagination. Electric sand, unexplored oceans, busy cities, full moons, clear golden sunsets, and an ongoing reference to life's spectrum of colour.

It was also a great tool to use my own surroundings as a reference for some settings. In the third chapter, I described the apartment I lived in, matching it with a movie-like scene. The magic glass elevator that has a mind of its own.

As I wrote the story, I continued to review the songs and interchange the lyrics, matching words and phrases to the story line. Maré Alta was a chill song I wrote referencing parts of the last chapter "Sail across The Sun" and I enjoyed staying up late at night playing it and thinking of my own personal growth. I gave it a portuguese name to remind me of my time in Brasil. I also changed some grooves of the instrumentation so the music would fit with the visions I had in each chapter. Coming back to Australia, Our new band was formed and the songs were arranged and finalised once again with band versions and acoustic versions. The songs continued to flow based on the story of the book and the 5 song project eventually became an 8 track album.

The last song I wrote was "A place to occupy". This was a break from the story of "Distant Echoes", and in my mind, it was based more on a spin off from the man on the rooftop in chapter 3. The song started as a relationship between two people stuck in an apartment and the man descending towards madness, not knowing how he got to where he was. Eventually he would meet the architect, share his wisdom of life, and disappear after free falling from the top of the rooftop.

The project took the good part of two years but eventually became something bigger than what I thought it could ever be.

When I finally finished, I realised that I hadn't just written a fictional story, but more of a philosophical adventure of life, told through the naivety of a dreamer wanting more.

We are all just dreamers living the perfect hallucination and we can become the architects of our own lives.

Distant Echoes E.P

Lyrics

Space Before Time

Verse

Breathe In
All of the lights

Hallucinating and craving
The space after time

She will keep waiting
Forever waiting

The Architect Of Dreams

Verse
I remember an ocean of strange colours
All running into one another, just desperate to feel something
A familiar scene of a place that I had never been
Maybe these lives were intertwined
By a web of my own memories

Chorus
They call you. The Architect that weaves
the lives in-between
And they think that you know nothing of what it's like to dream,
or to want to live
And it's so sweet and so deep in the way
that you love your designs
Now they have your mind

Verse
As I wandered this place of haunting mystery
A wave came and swept me away,
and held me at the bottom of the sea
There was a message that I knew I'd seen in another dream
Just constructed thoughts to give an effect,
that I was actually living

Chorus
They call you. The Architect that weaves,
 the lives in-between
And they think that you know nothing of what it's like to dream,
oh how you want to live
And it's so sweet and so deep in the way
that you love your designs
Now they have your mind

All I Ever Wanted

Verse
In the night, a silhouette
She creates the escape like no one can
Catch some light in a globe
Chase the time until it slows

We keep running and running
Running, running
We're running away

Chorus
It's all I ever wanted
Just to know what it's like, just to have a taste
It's all I ever wanted

Verse
Leave your thoughts by the water
Stare straight through the coloured lights
Let it go with the motion
All the things that make you alive

We keep running and running
Running, Running,Running
We keep running running
Are you alive

Chorus
It's all I ever wanted
Just to know what it's like, just to have a taste
It's all I ever wanted

In The Midst

Verse
I've been spending hours of my days
Watching the time as its fading away
The paradox remains the same
I held my breath as the sea would rise
Hiding away from times disguise
Distorting the sound of speeding light

Chorus
We were strangers from the start
Wandering here in the midst of it all
As space begins tearing us apart
I wonder
Just who's in control, who's in control

Verse
All of these nights I've been lying awake
Thinking of future situations I've made
And things that I could over complicate
All of the voices hiding under the bed
Battle between what was circumstance
And just what, remains coincidence

Chorus
We were strangers from the start
Wandering here in the midst of it all
As space begins tearing us apart
I wonder

Outro
Who's in control, Who's in control

A Place To Occupy

Verse
Lay down, all your plans so I can see them clear
I want to know, your resistance,
Bleed out, all the salt from where you've been
Show me something sweet and I'll surrender

Chorus
Now I'm stuck like honey
In the middle of two worlds,
What we know as our reality
And the place in my mind that you occupy
I see time is dancing
From the pictures you hang on the wall
Still I question the motif
Where we come from and where do we go

Verse
Lay down, all your records we can let them spin
The background seems so thin, when you're around
Breathe out, I'm intrigued by what you hold inside
The way you gaze through the cityscape
Finding patterns in the indigo sky

Chorus
Now I'm stuck like honey
In the middle of two worlds,
What we know as our reality
And the place in my mind that you occupy
Now I'm starting to realize
It's not me in those picture on the wall
Could you tell me how I got here
 Because I don't remember at all.

Moonlight

Verses
Driving all through the night
Take your place so easy
So trusting in the tides
As you kiss the breeze
I'll chase you down the seaside
To a little house by the shore
We were drifting with the moving lights
For a moment, we forgot where we were

You're talking in your sleep
Tell what you see
Would you tell me all those strange things
And all your fears
You've been sleeping at the wheel
Dreaming through your days
Now I fear, that the moonlight
Could take you away

You're talking in your sleep
Tell what you see
Would you tell me all those strange things
And all your fears
You've been sleeping at the wheel
Dreaming through your days
Now I fear that the moonlight
Could take you away
It could take us away

Maré Alta

Verse

If you hand me the gun
I'll shoot the sun down
I'll seek where she goes
Through the night
Just to find
That she's been waiting on the tides
She's been waiting on the tides
To turn
In my direction
For so long
She's been waiting on the tides
She's been waiting
For the turn of the tides

Sail Across The Sun

Verse
If I could sail across the sun, and find what was to become
Then I wouldn't have to wait, come and take me away
If I knew what there was to find, then how would I spend the life
Would I be satisfied, with the time

Chorus
If all these things could happen to the truth
Would I still be there on the shore, sitting next to you
If I was to stray a little further from the dream
Would you still be there on the shore
Waiting for me

Verse
If I could sail across the sun, to a land where nobody had gone
Discover things so profound, in the deepness of sound
If I got lost along the way, in the echoes of the day
Maybe I'd stay in that place so sweet

Chorus
If all these things could happen to the truth
Would I still be there on the shore, sitting next to you
If I was to stray a little further from the dream
Would you still be there on the shore,
Waiting for me

If I was to stray a little further from the dream
Would you still be there on the shore waiting for me
And if I had known, all along
How could I have known, that you would wait for me
You're always waiting for me

www.ingramcontent.com/pod-product-compliance
Lightning Source LLC
Chambersburg PA
CBHW070828220526
45466CB00002B/777